A to Z Virtues for Kids

26 Powerful Examples of Virtue in Action

Chaz E. Allen

Published by Challenge My Family, 2019.

A TO Z VIRTUES FOR KIDS

First edition. September 17, 2019.

Copyright © 2019 Chaz E. Allen.

Written by Chaz E. Allen.

To the five towhead kids who make every day an adventure. I love you RASCALS.

Introduction

We need heroes. We need examples of what right looks like, where we can see a principle put into action and then observe the results. The farmers law is immutable and eternally true.

"You reap what you sow."

What are the consequences of a life lived with audacity, integrity, and thankfulness? We can look to Patton, Regulus, and Helen Keller to find out. What is the outcome if we persevere, and live nobly, with zeal? Ed Coan, George Washington, and Amelia Earhart show us.

They say, you sow a thought; you reap an action. You sow an action; you reap a habit. You sow a habit; you reap your character. You sow your character; you reap a legacy. I hope to see my children and this whole generation reap a legacy worth reading about, a legacy of virtue and hope.

I encourage every family to read about one of these examples, talk about the virtue in question, and then discuss how their child can apply it to their daily life—whether that be in school, on the soccer field, or at home. This is also a workbook, so at the end of each section please use the space provided to make some goals that you can pursue. Then, continue on and do some more research into the life of the historic figure, see what more there is to gain.

Best,

Chaz E. Allen

1. AUDACITY of Patton

Intrepid boldness, strong confidence in yourself.

"L'audace, l'audace, toujours l'audace!" ("Audacity, audacity, always audacity!") –
Napoleon Bonaparte

DURING WORLD WAR II, a small band of paratroopers (soldiers that jump out of airplanes) were surrounded in a town called Bastogne. Everyone thought they were going to be captured or even destroyed by their brutal enemy—German Nazis.

General George S. Patton wouldn't let that happen. He was AUDACIOUS and turned his forces north and moved hundreds of miles over heavily forested terrain, in the dead of winter to save the American soldiers.

He attacked with two full divisions of tanks and infantry within forty-eight hours and saved the day. Patton had AUDACITY.

I CAN BE MORE AUDACIOUS by...

2. BENEVOLENCE of Mandela

The quality of being well-meaning; kindness.

"Courageous people do not fear forgiving, for the sake of peace." -Nelson Mandela

T he Apartheid made living in South Africa a terrible place if you were not a white European. Black people were heavily discriminated. They had to use separate bathrooms, faucets, park benches, entrances. Instead of comfy office jobs, they were forced to labor in the dangerous and dirty gold and diamond mines.

After a revolution President Nelson Mandela, a black man, came to power. Instead of seeking revenge, he was BENEVOLENT and created a program called Truth and Reconciliation.

The program helped everyone find peace and enter the future with a far more positive direction. Mandela had BENEVOLENCE.

I WILL BE MORE BENEVOLENT tomorrow, I will...

3. CANDOR of Hackworth

The quality of being frank, open, and sincere.

"If you don't like something, don't snivel or whimper about it. Sound off – express your views – be prepared for the consequences." -COL David Hackworth

The steamy jungle of Vietnam was a tough place for a soldier to fight. The North Vietnamese Army was stealthy and resilient, a very worthy adversary. American forces fought for years and years trying to defeat an insurgency that could not be defeated by bullets, bombs, or napalm (a jelly-like fuel that can burn up miles of jungle at a time).

LTC "Hack" Hackworth felt that the combat tactics and techniques we were using to measure success in the war were not working. Instead of keeping silent to make his boss happy, he had CANDOR. He spoke up and shared his observations and ideas.

When his leaders would not listen, he appeared on a major news network. Hackworth's CANDID comments helped bring that bloody war to a close.

I WILL USE MORE CANDOR when I speak with...

4. DISCIPLINE at Rorke's Drift

The ability to control yourself, even in difficult situations.

"An army is a fighting weapon molded by discipline and controlled by leaders; the essence of the army is discipline." – Bernard Montgomery

Rorke's Drift was a tiny outpost in Africa. Only around 200 British soldiers defended it. The local Zulu Warriors were not happy with Britain's presence in their lands and sent an army to destroy them.

Over 4,000 Zulu warriors attacked the tiny British force. They fought all day and into the night. DISCIPLINE led the troops to overcome their fears and hold their position, firing aimed shots from their rifles.

Sensing that their tenacious opponent would not break ranks, the Zulu eventually retreated. DISCIPLINE helped the British soldiers hold their ground and survive against a far larger opponent.

I WILL SHOW DISCIPLINE as I...

5. EQUANIMITY of Bogle

Mental calmness, composure, evenness of temper.

"Time is your friend; impulse is your enemy." -Jack Bogle

Investing in the stock market is a very good way to help your money grow. Each dollar invested in stocks becomes a little green soldier who is working to earn you more money both day and night, 365 days a year.

Still, the market is volatile and sometimes you can lose money when you invest if you sell when prices are low. Financial managers move your money around and sometimes charge excessive fees.

Jack Bogle took a different approach and designed an index fund. It has super low fees and allows you to own a tiny piece of thousands of businesses. With EQUANIMITY, like Bogle, you will make money—a lot of money—in the long run.

I WILL DEMONSTRATE equanimity the next time...

6. FRUGALITY of Franklin

Quality of being economical with money; thriftiness.

"A penny saved is a penny earned."-Ben Franklin

BENJAMIN FRANKLIN WAS one of America's Forefathers. He was an author, printer, scientist, and inventor. He wrote the Poor Richard's Almanac that offered great advice on how to be thrifty.

FRUGALITY helped Benjamin Franklin acquire much wealth. He used his considerable resources to support the American Revolution.

He was a colonial era renaissance man; he never spent his money on lavish living or excessive luxuries. Franklin was FRUGAL.

I WILL BE MORE FRUGAL the next time I...

7. GRIT of Murphy

Courage and resolve; strength of character.

G

"The way I see it, if you're scared of something, you'd better get busy and do something about it. I'd call that a challenge—and I believe that the way to grow is to meet all the challenges as they come along."- Audie Murphy

A udie Murphy was not a big muscle-bound warrior. He was so small the military recruiters actually turned him away when he tried to enlist for World War II. That would not stop Audie, he was a fighter. He had GRIT.

He wanted to go and defend the free world from Nazi totalitarianism (that's a harsh form of government that severely controls its people). During a vicious battle in France, Audie single handedly fought off an entire Nazi company of soldiers.

Wounded and out of ammunition, he led a successful counterattack. Audie's GRIT helped him win the day.

GRIT WILL HELP ME SUCCEED in...

8. HUMILITY of Aurelius

Modest opinion of one's own importance & abilities.

"The first rule is to keep an untroubled spirit. The second is to look things in the face and know them for what they are." -Marcus Aurelius

MARCUS AURELIAS WAS the emperor of Rome during its zenith (that means its peak or highest point, when Rome was at its very best). He was called Caesar and ruled his people with benevolence and fairness.

Aurelias was also a warrior-philosopher. He led many battles against barbarians that sought to invade and defeat Rome. HUMILITY helped the emperor listen to his generals and centurions (the soldiers that commanded his legions).

Caesar was the most powerful man in Rome, in all the world even. Still Aurelius chose to be HUMBLE.

I WILL BE MORE HUMBLE as I...

9. INTEGRITY of Regulus

Abiding by strong moral principles; state of being whole.

"Your word is your bond." – Unknown

MARCUS ATILIUS REGULUS was a Roman general in the Punic Wars long ago. He led successful campaigns against the Carthaginians. Sadly, he was captured after a very big battle. He was thrown in prison and the war continued.

The Carthaginians started to lose the war, so they offered Regulus a deal. He could go on parole (the temporary release of a prisoner for a specific purpose) and see his family. There were conditions though, he had to represent Carthage before the Roman senate and—above all—he had to return to Carthage afterwards.

Regulus had INTEGRITY and went home and gave an honest account of his observations to the senate. Then, to many people's surprise, he returned to Carthage even though he knew it might lead to torture and death. Regulus was a man of his word, he had INTEGRITY.

I WILL DEMONSTRATE integrity by...

10. JUSTICE of Crazy Horse

The condition of being morally correct or fair.

"Upon suffering beyond suffering, the Red Nation shall rise again, and it shall be a blessing for a sick world. A world filled with broken promises, selfishness and separations. The world longs for light again."- Crazy Horse

IN THE WILD WEST OF the United States, two brave warriors faced off in the Montana plains. It was Crazy Horse with an alliance of Sioux tribes against Colonel George Armstrong Custer with a small band of cavalrymen.

Custer was there under orders from the U.S. Army to try and make the West safe for pioneer settlers. Crazy Horse was fighting for JUSTICE for his people.

Sadly, the American government broke its promises to the indigenous people too many times and forced the tribes from their lands. Crazy Horse fought fiercely and won the battle because he felt his cause was JUST.

I WILL BE JUST WITH my fellow...

11. KNOWLEDGE of Carson

Understanding obtained by experience or study.

K

"There is a tendency of people to try to make you believe only a few people are smart. As a brain surgeon, I know better than that." – Ben Carson

Ben Carson grew up in a rough part of Detroit. His family was poor and his mom had to work extra hard to take care of him and his brother. Their dad had abandoned them when he was young.

His mom demanded a lot of him. She would not let him watch television and made him write not just one, but two book reports every week. She wanted her sons to gain KNOWLEDGE because she knew that knowledge is power.

Ben did not always like the extra work, but now he is very grateful for his mother. He went to school at a prestigious university and became a world-renowned neurosurgeon. Dr. Ben Carson's knowledge allowed him to help countless people and make the world a better place.

I WILL GAIN KNOWLEDGE as I study...

12. LOYALTY of Crockett

Faithful to a cause, ideal, custom, or institution; allegiance.

"Loyalty to the country always. Loyalty to the government when it deserves it."–
Mark Twain

D avey Crockett was known as the king of the wild frontier. After a life of trapping and hunting he went to Washington to serve as a member of congress. LOYALTY to his honor and his nation led him to stand against unjust policies like the Indian Removal Act.

After Washington, he went to Texas to help them win their independence from Mexico. He fought alongside Jim Bowie (he made the large Bowie knife famous) at the Alamo.

Mexico's forces eventually overran the Alamo's meager fort and all of its defenders lost their lives. Texas later won its independence. When Texans yelled "Remember the Alamo" they remembered the LOYALTY of men like Crockett.

I CAN SHOW LOYALTY by...

13. MODERATION of Rickenbacker

Avoidance of excess or extremes in behavior & opinion.

"Moderation in all things is the best policy." -Plautus

Eddie Rickenbacker flew airplanes in World War I. He became America's greatest fighter ace (that means he shot down a lot of enemy aircraft). He did not start out as a fighter pilot though, he actually started with racing cars. He even competed in the famous Indianapolis 500.

After the great war, he became a successful businessman. When World War II broke out, he agreed to carry a message to an American General in the Pacific.

Unfortunately, his airplane got lost at sea and had to ditch in the water. MODERATION of their supplies helped him and his crew survive for twenty-four whole days at sea, before they were rescued. A successful racecar driver, pilot, and businessman, Rickenbacker led a life of excellence and MODERATION.

I WILL FIND MODERATION when it comes to...

14. NOBILITY of Washington

Quality of having high moral qualities or character; royal heritage.

"The harder the conflict, the greater the triumph." -George Washington

WHEN THE AMERICAN COLONIES decided they wanted to fight for their independence from the Empire of Britain, they knew they would need a leader for their fledgling army. The continental congress unanimously chose George Washington. He was a NOBLE leader who earned the respect of soldier, civilian, and politician alike.

At the battle of Trenton, he led his army on a secret mission across the Delaware river on Christmas night. He named it operation Victory or Death.

He NOBLY led the colonial forces against crack Hessian mercenaries (those are soldiers-for-hire that fight for the highest bidder) and emerged victorious. Washington later became America's first president.

I WILL ACT MORE NOBLY when I am at...

15. ORDERLINESS of the Cosmos

Diligent cleanliness, being well arranged and organized.

"There is an orderliness in the universe, there is an unalterable law governing everything and every being that exists or lives. It is no blind law; for no blind law can govern the conduct of living beings." – Ghandi

DID YOU KNOW THE MOON is 238,900 miles away from Earth? Neil Armstrong traveled all of those miles to the moon in a spaceship. When his moon lander set down at Tranquility Base, he descended its steps and said, "That's one small step for a man, one giant leap for mankind."

He became the first man to set foot on the moon. He proved that mankind has the capacity to achieve the impossible.

While looking out at the vast solar system before him he noted the ORDER-LINESS of the universe. There is an ORDER to things that will inspire awe in anyone willing to see it.

I WILL HELP MY HOUSE be more orderly by...

16. PERSEVERANCE of Ed Coan

Persistence despite difficulty or delay in achieving success.

"The key to powerlifting success is regular, long term, repeated behavior."- Ed Coan

E d Coan was an unlikely powerlifting champion. At 5'6" he did not have the gigantic muscles and height of most of his competition. Still, he was determined to be the strongest possible version of himself and PERSERVERANCE helped him win the World Championship competition.

He did not just win it once, he won it over and over again and set 71 world records that stood for more than 20 years. What Lebron James is to basketball and Tiger Woods is to golf, Ed Coan is to powerlifting—except on an even higher scale.

PERSERVERANCE and hard training helped him achieve the gargantuan numbers of a 1,000 pound squat, 585 bench press and 901 deadlift. Coan was the greatest powerlifter of all time.

I WILL PERSEVERE BY...

17. QUIETNESS of Christ

Absence of noise or bustle; state of calm, tranquility, and peace.

"Peace I give unto you...let not your heart be troubled, neither let it be afraid." -Jesus Christ

J esus Christ lived in ancient Israel and was a powerful teacher. He QUIETLY brought people closer to God and gave them a deeper sense of meaning and purpose.

Sadducees and Pharisees (the local religious leaders of the day) did not like his teachings and wanted to stop him. They tried to trap him with his own words and get him in trouble by asking him very tough questions.

Sometimes, instead of answering angrily he would use QUIETNESS to calm the situation. Jesus became known as the Prince of Peace.

I WILL BE MORE QUIET the next time I...

18. RESPONSIBILITY of Curie

Ability to act correctly and make decisions on your own; your duty.

"Nothing in life is to be feared, it is only to be understood. Now is the time to understand more, so that we may fear less." – Marie Curie

Marie Curie was a scientist back in a time when very few women were able to become scientists or even get an education. She was determined, though. She felt a RESPONSIBILITY to contribute to science and medicine.

Despite the naysayers (that's people who criticize and make fun of you) she pioneered the field of radioactivity. She earned the Nobel Peace Prize—two of them!—for her contribution.

RESPONSIBILITY led Marie to do what she felt was her duty. Many people who suffered from cancer were saved by the medical application of her research into radiation.

I WILL SHOW RESPONSIBILITY by...

19. SPARTAN Leonidas

Indifference to comfort or luxury, strict self-discipline; laconic.

"Be brave my heart. Plant your feet and square your shoulders to the enemy. Meet him among the man-killing spears. Hold your ground. In victory, do not brag. In defeat, do not weep." -Archilochus

COULD YOU IMAGINE BEING in a battle and outnumbered 1,000 to one? For seven whole days, 300 Spartans (and a handful of Greeks) held off a massive army of 300,000 Persians at Thermopylae—The Hot Gates.

It was a narrow pass that required the enemy to funnel their forces toward the awaiting SPARTAN shields. Leonidas led the 300 and was a great warrior.

He and his people lived simple lives and were concise in their speech. They chose their values carefully and stuck to them. They did not value luxury or fine architecture like other societies. No, they were warriors that chose a SPARTAN life and scoffed at a life of ease.

I WILL BE MORE SPARTAN by...

20. THANKFULLNESS of Keller

Feeling of being happy or grateful; showing appreciation.

"When one door of happiness closes, another opens; but often we look so long at the closed door that we do not see the one which has been opened for us." – Helen Keller

WHAT WOULD IT BE LIKE to not hear or see anything? Go ahead and try it. Close your eyes and cover your ears. That was what life was like for Helen Keller ever since Scarlet Fever left her blind and deaf as a baby. She later said it felt like she was at sea in a dense fog.

Her parents loved her and tried to help her communicate. They eventually sought the help Anne Sullivan—a special teacher. Helen was THANKFUL for her new teacher and, after much toil, she learned how to communicate using sign language.

Helen went on to study at a university and became a famous speaker. She was a beacon of positivity and THANKFULNESS in the world.

I AM THANKFUL FOR...

21. UNITY of Vasco

State of being joined together, in agreement; oneness, harmony.

"Ó mar salgado, quanto do teu sal São lágrimas de Portugal!... Valeu a pena? Tudo vale a pena. Se a alma não é pequena." (Oh salted sea, how much of your waters are tears from Portugal? ...Is it worth it? Everything is worth it if the soul is not weak.)
– Fernando Pessoa

Have you ever seen the ocean? It is vast and deep. Long ago, in Portugal, many sailors ventured out into the ocean to try and discover a sea route to the rich markets of India.

Many ships and sailors were lost to the turbulent sea, never to return home. Nonetheless, an age of discovery UNITED the Portuguese people and Vasco da Gama led a small fleet to yet again try and sail to India. They had to go around Africa and the Cape of Storms.

It was incredibly difficult. Two ships sank and many drowned but UNITY helped the crews brave the storms and survive. Da Gama made it to India and the tip of Africa was renamed the Cape of Good Hope.

I WILL SHOW UNITY AS I...

22. VALOR of Shughart and Gordon

Boldness or determination in facing great danger; heroic courage.

"The only thing necessary for the triumph of evil is for good men to do nothing." — Edmund Burke

S hughart and Gordan were Delta Force soldiers assigned to protect their comrades in Somalia. On a fateful mission, not just one, but two helicopters were shot down in the African city of Mogadishu.

Almost all of the rescuers were trying to get to the first crash site when the second helicopter was hit. No one would be able to help the second crew and they would soon be captured or killed by local warlord militias.

Shughart and Gordan VALOROUSLY requested to fast rope in (that's sliding down a rope out of a helicopter) so they could protect the injured crew. They were heavily outnumbered and knew the odds, but still chose to go in. Though they both fought with VALOR, they eventually perished in the fight. They did save the life of one of the pilots.

I WILL DEMONSTRATE valor the next time that I...

23. WIT of Roosevelt

Ability to use words in an amusing, intelligent way; mental sharpness.

"Don't hit a man at all if you can avoid it, but if you have to hit him, knock him out." – Teddy Roosevelt

Teddy Roosevelt was born into a wealthy family. Instead of sitting on a comfy couch having servants bring him tea, he ventured out into the West and became a cowboy.

He also became the Governor of New York City and walked the streets with the police. Later, he volunteered to become a Colonel in the Spanish-American War.

His variety of experiences gave him WIT as he inspired his men. He said, "The only man who never makes a mistake is the man who never does anything." He and his men charged up San Juan Hill together and helped America win the war. Eventually, he became the President of the United States and he became known as a tough, WITTY leader.

I WILL TRY AND BE MORE witty by...

24. XENIAL Alexander the Great

Hospitable, especially to visiting guests or foreigners; friendly host.

"Whatever possession we gain by our sword cannot be sure or lasting, but the love gained by kindness and moderation is certain and durable." – Alexander the Great

A lexander the Great was a young man when he campaigned with his Macedonian Phalanxes (that's a formation where all the soldiers form up in a square and interlock their shields).

He and his army conquered the entire known world in just a few short years. In those days, it was common for a conqueror to kill the local leaders and try to eliminate local religions.

Alexander was different, he was XENIAL and respected the customs and traditions of his people. He let them rule themselves and was a XENIAL, benevolent emperor.

I WILL BE A XENIAL host the next time that...

25. YOUTHFULNESS of Mothers

Vigor, freshness, and vitality as associated with being young.

"Motherhood is crazy and chaotic. It's survival of the fittest most days. I've learned kids can either give you grey hairs or spark youthfulness inside you. It's up to you how you want to age." -Sara Allen

Mothers have to do a lot in a family. Can you name all of the things that your mom does for you? In our house, Sara wears many hats.

She is a chef, a mentor, a maid, a manager, an accountant, a spiritual leader, a teacher, a disciplinarian, and a YOUTHFUL friend. Even though she has a lot to do every day, she takes the time to play with her sweet children.

Many mothers, the world over, give their very all to help their families. They still retain a YOUTHFUL spirit. (You should probably give your mom a kiss!)

I CAN DEMONSTRATE YOUTHFULNESS by...

26. ZEAL of Earhart

Great energy or enthusiasm in the pursuit of a cause or an objective.

"Never interrupt someone doing something you said couldn't be done." – Amelia Earhart

Airplanes are amazing inventions. They defy gravity, fly in the air, and do amazing acrobatics. Years ago, only men flew airplanes, but Amelia Earhart did not want to miss out on the fun.

She studied and trained extra hard and became an incredible pilot. She pursued her passion for aviation with ZEAL. She broke many records and, in 1928, even became the first woman to cross the Atlantic Ocean all by herself.

She was a pioneer in aviation. Her ZEALOUSNESS paved the way for many women to enter into the world of professional flying.

I WILL BE ZEALOUS AS I...

About the Author

Chaz Allen is the proud father of five marvelous children. He is also a Soldier. During two combat deployments to Afghanistan as a scout helicopter pilot, he developed a passion for writing. The letters he sent home gave him a chance to communicate with his family and share experiences. Not only that, it allowed him to make observations, offer counsel, and ponder life's lessons. He wants to see the rising generation fulfill their potential and make the world an even better place.

He is a graduate of the United States Military Academy and holds a Master's degree from the University of Utah. Ranger, Sapper, Airborne, Air Assault, SERE, and Army Aviation Training gave him an appreciation for lifelong learning. His wife, Sara Allen, remains his inspiration and closest friend.

Read more at challengemyfamily.com.

Made in the USA
Lexington, KY
14 November 2019